To my mother, grandmother, daughters, and generations to come.

Preface

Growing up, I loved watching movies. I was amazed by how actors and actresses completely "became" their characters. Every facial expression and body movement drew me into their stories. Though I knew the characters were not real, I often wondered, "How do they do this? How do they become so good at playing these roles? How do they pretend to be someone they really aren't?" Sometimes, actors and actresses play their roles so well that we can't tell the difference between their on-screen personas and their real-life selves.

I remember being around elderly family members who would tell us that we couldn't use the word "lie." Instead, we had to say, "telling stories." That's what actors and actresses did—they told stories. But they weren't lying, were they? Yet, deep down, I realized that performing is a form of deception. It's about presenting a version of ourselves or portraying a character that may not align with our true identity.

As I grew into my own acting abilities, I became aware of the difference between performance and truth. Actors and performers immerse themselves in roles, sometimes blurring the line between reality and fiction. In doing so, they deceive themselves and invite others to believe with them.

However, this raises deeper questions about the nature of performance. Are we performers because we have a God-given talent that we want to share with the world, or are we performing because we have something to prove?

This distinction shapes not just how we tell stories, but also why we tell them—and whether, in the act of performance, we are ultimately lying to ourselves and others about who we truly are.

Actor: noun: plural noun: actors*

1. a person whose profession is acting on the stage, in movies, or on television or a person who behaves in a way that is not genuine.*

Genuine: adjective

1. truly what something is said to be; authentic.

According to these definitions, an actor must behave in a disingenuous way to portray a role believable to their audience. The difference between us and our favorite television stars is that they do it purely for entertainment and the enjoyment of their fans. Why do ordinary people like us do it? Most of us don't have a fan base or aren't making millions by pretending. Are we performers because we have a God-given talent that we want to show the world, or are we performing because we are seeking validation due to our intrusive thoughts of inferiority? What do we really have to prove when we are already enough?

Truth Lies Delusions

Truth Lies Delusions

Truth Lies Delusions

Disclaimer:

The stories shared in this memoir are my truths and reflect my real-life experiences. The information disclosed may be shocking, disturbing, and triggering to some readers. All individuals and scenarios in this book are based on real experiences. Reader discretion is advised. If you or someone you know is experiencing suicidal thoughts, domestic violence, drug addiction, or a mental health crisis, please reach out to someone you trust or use the resources available to you. Remember, the world is a better place with you in it.

Suicide Prevention Lifeline

800-273-8255

National Hotline for Mental Health Crises and Suicide Prevention

Dial 988

Domestic Violence Hotline

1-800-799-7233
1-800-787-3224 (TTY)

National Drug and Substance Abuse Hotline

844-289-0879

Contents

1. Innocence
2. The Performer
3. The Performer and The Fighter
4. The Studious One and The Rebellious One
5. The Vixen and The Fighter
6. The Perfect Mother
7. The "Holier Than Thou" Church Girl
8. The "Perfect" Wife
9. Everything to Everybody
10. Hard Lessons Learned

Chapter 1

Innocence

As a child, I remember pastors, parents, grandparents, and other elders saying, "Tell the truth and shame the devil! The truth shall set you free!" Of course, all of it went in one ear and out the other. Truth be told, I was actually afraid of telling the truth because the same people who encouraged me to tell the truth were the same ones to reprimand me whenever I did. Telling the truth may have been as simple as, "Yes, Ma'am. I forgot my homework again," or "Ma, I hate sweet peas!" But it never seemed to turn out the way they told me it would. It was never that easy. Somehow, I still ended up getting fussed at for speaking up and telling the truth.

The man who stepped in and stepped up as my *father, Tim,* taught me to accept responsibility for my wrongs and own my mistakes to free me from any guilt. He'd say, "Ciera, just tell the truth. Don't carry the guilt of telling a lie." See, the thing about a lie is it eats away at you like an infestation. It wears you down until you can no longer carry it. A lie cannot remain hidden. It starts as a tiny seed but continues to grow until it is forced to deliver the truth.

My mother was sixteen years old when she got pregnant by my twenty-year-old father. She knew there were people who would not want me to exist. She knew she would be forced to abort her love child. To guarantee my survival, she and my dad kept their little secret from the world for six months. During this time, my mom sharpened her skills as a performer. She learned to mask her fear with a smile and pretend that everything was normal. For six months, she hid her growing belly behind the curtain of her sister's oversized clothes. She, literally, covered up the truth... she manipulated and lied to her family... just to protect me. As I grew in her womb, I was marinated in deceit.

When my grandmother found out about the pregnancy, she demanded my mother to have an abortion. Thankfully, the plan to hide me worked because the pregnancy was too far along to terminate. The truth was positioning itself for birth. My father, now twenty-one years old, ran from the reality that he would soon become a father. On January 31, 1989, my mother gave birth. Shortly after I was born, my parents tried to work things out until it didn't. I was only a couple months old when my father abandoned me. Growing up, I didn't understand the impact of being abandoned, but my spirit felt the divide. My heart was split like the curtains for an opening act. This is where the performance began as I shadowed my mother to become the leading actress.

As a toddler, I was my mother's little princess. I admired everything about her. She dressed me in the prissiest little outfits and styled my curly hair with the fanciest bows. I was her perfect little baby doll. My father's marriage to another woman solidified the end of my mother's desire to rekindle the love between them. She had to face the harsh reality that she needed to move on. She introduced me to another man who would play the supporting role as my father for the next two years. Our dynamic duo suddenly turned into a family of three and then four. On September 8, 1990, I was introduced to a new baby sister. I was actually excited about having a little sister to play with. Now, I had my own baby doll, just like my mommy.

My mother's new relationship quickly became toxic from the emotional and physical abuse which eventually projected onto me and my sister. See, my mother has always been a fighter. Having a mother addicted to crack cocaine and a father addicted to alcohol and heroin conditioned my mom to always be on guard. Friends tried to support her, and her grandparents provided as much support as they could, but there was an invisible villain that only my mom could only see.

She could never really explain what she was fighting, but she had this mentality that it was her against the world. Trying to protect my sister and me from living the life she had, she became very controlling and overbearing. Life was hard. Yet, someway, somehow my mother always found a way to provide for us.

Two more romantic, but toxic and abusive relationships followed. At this point, my biological father was only a phantom of my imagination. I watched my mother balance the responsibilities of raising two daughters with the support of her grandparents, working a full-time job, and attending school as a first-generation college student. In all honesty, I began to admire the fight that once traumatized me.

Life seemed to be on the up and up. My mom earned her degree, had a manager's position at Burger King, and eventually became a first-time home builder and buyer. Church became a regular part of our life. My sister and I even joined a children's choir. Although we were the youngest and smallest in the choir, we learned quickly how to rock and sway to the music. I knew when the choir director took her position, it was showtime! My mother also joined a young-adult choir to help develop her relationship with God. Little did she know, these "Friends in Christ" lead to a relationship that she was not looking for. Tim was tall, dark, and handsome and had a voice smooth as silk. While all eyes were on him, his eyes were fixed on my mama's fuchsia lipstick. She was the least bit interested… well, at least in front of everyone else. On stage she was poised, but behind the scenes, she wanted him just as much as he wanted her. It was a struggle. She knew her focus should be on her two daughters, but there was something different about this man; something she had never experienced.

My mom soon discovered that Tim had a daughter. It was a spring Sunday afternoon, the choir had finished singing their staple song, "Safe In His Arms" during the choir's anniversary when my mother introduced us to Tim's daughter. She held on tight to her father's leg as she stared at us with her thick, raised eyebrows. She made it very clear that this was HER daddy! I didn't see her as a threat. I actually admired her. I loved everything about her. She had thick, beautiful ponytails that laid perfectly on the shoulders of her floral dress. Her smile seemed to stretch from ear-to-ear drawing attention to her dangling earrings. I thought everything about her was cool. Tim had a daughter, and I was excited. There was somebody else I could play dolls with and ride bikes. Every time we saw Tim, we saw his daughter. He was loving, nurturing, and attentive to her needs. He was present. Maybe this is what made him different. He was present.

Seeing Tim interact with his daughter was an attraction to my mom. This is the special quality that she had always looked for in a man; to be present for his child. As their relationship strengthened, our family of three grew to four. He moved in. This was different for me because I was not used to a man being in the house full-time. Tim taught me how to ride a bike, throw a football, and he even pretended to enjoy our quirky made - up dance routines. He felt like a dad. I can remember my sister and I asking if he could be our dad. He gladly accepted. All the while, I still longed for the love and acceptance from my biological father. Tim was present, but my dad left a void that could not be filled by any man.

Things began to move quickly between Tim and my mom. Not long after he moved in, she announced she was pregnant with twins! By now, Tim's daughter was practically living with us. Our small, three bedroom, one bathroom home was bursting by the seams. On June 29, 1995, the twins arrived. Our family of five became a family of seven. I was forced from having my own room to the bottom bunk of an overcrowded bedroom just to make room for the twins' cribs and my new sister's pristine daybed. My perspective of this "happy little family" began to shift. The admiration for my new big sister turned into envy. She took over my room and my little sister. I didn't feel like I fit anymore. I didn't laugh at their jokes. I didn't dance to their beat. I didn't play their silly games. I didn't want to ride bikes, and I certainly didn't want to play with their stupid dolls. This new "sister" was taking over! My position as first was pushed to second, and then forced to last. She even took my mother's attention. She was like an understudy who took my role. Although I was in a home full of kids and chaos, loneliness was the loudest thing in the room.

Chapter 2

The Performer

Just a few months after the twins were born, my mother married the man of her dreams. On November 11, 1995, I stood in the middle as one of her three flower girls. They exchanged vows and rings as a commitment to each other. Then, they placed rings on our little fingers to symbolize our blended family becoming one. A platform of bridesmaids and groomsmen were in awe of our "perfect little family".

Our family never had a dull moment. We couldn't afford much but we made the best out of life. Weekends and summers were filled with water balloon fights, sledding down the back steps, making dance and fight videos, and any other free activity my mother could come up with. We seemed to be adjusting well to this new family dynamic. A few years into the marriage, our parents shocked us with the news of another sibling. Tim had another daughter. What? Where will she sleep? By now, I was eleven years old and at the start of puberty! This little house couldn't hold anymore estrogen!

Everybody seemed to have found their place in the family except me. Where did I fit? I'm my mother's oldest but it doesn't feel like it. How did it change from being just Mommy and me to the black Brady Bunch? Even with all of the fun and excitement of having a big family, ironically, the only time I felt like number one was when I was alone. All of these kids and personalities came with different needs and demands for my mother's attention. Crying served no purpose. Besides, who would even see my tears? I just told myself, "Suck it up. It's going to be ok." I learned to adjust, adapt and figure things out on my own.

I felt invisible. Maybe this is how they all wanted it. Maybe I should run away. Maybe I should be dead. I rehearsed this mental monologue throughout my youth and teenage years. The thought of them losing me would definitely be easier than living a life that no one cared about. I never shared these thoughts with anyone because I knew it was not okay. I masked my feelings with drawing and sketching, but behind the scenes I was perfecting my craft of performing.

I found my place in my own imagination and my own space. I discovered that I could draw, sing, and dance in the privacy of my cramped bedroom. "Maybe this is something I can do to get attention", I thought. So, I performed for the family. They had no choice but to see me now! Besides, this is something none of my siblings could do. "Look what I drew! Look at my dance! Listen to my song!" The short attention of my mother and father proved that my performances were still not enough to validate me. "Ok, Cece, That's good. Go sit down." I ignored their request and thought, "Nope! While I have the attention, I plan to keep it!" I was determined to have more than 15 seconds of fame. I made a vow that one day, the name Ciera Sharde' would be in lights!

It hurt to see their attention quickly pulled to the demands of the other children. To cope, I lived in my dreams of one day becoming a star! In my childlike mind, I would be a model, a fashion designer, a movie star, an artist, a singer, and work at Burger King just like my mama.

Going through puberty was hard as hell. My emotions were all over the place and my body was drastically reacting to the hormonal changes. I was in the 6th grade when I started my period. I was so embarrassed when I bled through my shorts but too afraid to tell my mom. I was haunted by the old folks saying, "Starting your period too early means that girl is fast!". I wasn't fast at all. I just wanted to be mommy's little girl. Should I tell her, or should she already know? When I was younger, she noticed everything that changed about me; my clothes, my hair, and even my attitude. But now, she's too busy to see me at all. Does she even notice the difference in my breast? How do I handle all of these changes? My mom had somewhat prepared us about caring for our bodies, but never too in depth. I guess this was her way of keeping us "pure" and not revealing too many details about womanhood; something she had to learn from her own harsh realities.

During high school, I began to blossom in more ways than one. Not only was I physically developing, but my talents were also developing. I joined an art club, was flourishing on the church drama team, entered school talent shows, and even auditioned for a modeling competition. I may have been timid behind the scenes, but when they called for "lights, camera, and action", I owned the stage. I learned to be the perfectionist and performer everybody expected for me to be. Most importantly, I wanted my mother to be proud of me and possibly have my father finally show up for me. The applause and the standing ovations made me come alive. Every time they yelled my name, I performed more! I loved the feeling of being the center of attention. I was addicted to being "The Performer".

A real flex is just being yourself in a world where people live for an image.

  -unknown

CHAPTER 3

The Performer and The Fighter

My mother can tell you; I was afraid of just about any and everything. I was scared of the dark, heights, fireworks, and other loud noises, camera flashes but interesting enough, I wasn't too afraid of other people. I've always had a tenacious streak, and I wasn't one to back down from any challenge. One of my favorite lines and the most famous lines in the history of film was "All my life I had to fight." Some of us laugh because it's a staple inside joke in the black community. I laugh along with the rest of us, yet it brings so much truth to my story. People that know me from the outside looking in may say, "Child please… you don't know nothing about having to fight" and some of my family members may say the same. The fact of the matter is World War I ,World War II, and Vietnam were all 3 different wars with different types of casualties but that doesn't make one less gruesome than the other. Everyone has their fight in life, some may be internal, some may be spiritual, and some may be physical. Whether you are brawling in a nightclub or silently fighting demons in your mind, trust and believe we all have lived our Sofia in "The Color Purple" moments.

Being in school was quite traumatizing and the only safe place was my room with my art supplies, my music, my Barbie dolls and my favorite television shows. I remember in elementary school my 3rd grade teacher was tough. I was always talkative, and I always seemed to get distracted. I remember I was given practice tests for standardized testing, and I got tired and bored from the assignment. I chose to clean out my backpack and my drawing and colorings supplies and proceeded to do what I wanted to do. The thing about me is that when I am done with something or someone and I have my mind made up on the choices I want to make, nine times out of ten you are not going to convince me to do otherwise. My teacher came and redirected me, and I refused to listen. She fussed at me and walked me to the office to call my mother. I was rebelling because in that moment I was already tired of performing. My mother set a high expectation with her belt when I got home that day. I was angry and I felt like I had let my mother down. I understood my mother's expectations and although that was my truth in that moment I couldn't tell it. I knew what the right choice was and because I couldn't stand my teacher, and I was over the boring class assignments I chose to do otherwise. I was impulsive and stubborn but as a child I didn't realize that was not the time to bring World War II on my teacher. The following year I was in the 4th grade. That's where the fight began. I had a crush on a little boy in my class. We became friends and talked to each other daily. I decided that I would write him a love note and we would become boyfriend and girlfriend. I was confident that he would fall for me, and we would be on the playground happily ever after. Except… my 4th grade daydream turned into a nightmare. I shyly slipped him the note and he read it and laughed in my face. The next day our friendship became a horror story. I was told I had a big nose, and they called me names. I was told I was ugly and too skinny daily. Other boys from the class started to jump on the bandwagon and I felt the same pain and rejection all over again from when my biological father left. I began to fight and get suspended from school because I felt like I had to prove a point and protect myself. I was told by teachers, "oh boys only do that because they like you." and "they only act like that because they don't know how to tell you they think you're pretty." Although I had an amazing example from my new dad, The only other thing I really knew about love and relationships is that men get you pregnant and leave. All the other relationships my mother had before were toxic and the men were abusive. I knew that men hitting women was wrong but why was boys hitting girls excused? I told myself I would never end up abused like my mom and my grandmother. Throughout middle school I was constantly fighting to prove myself and everyone around me that I was not to be played with. I was found myself in the principal's office just about my whole 6th and 7th grade year because I was playing the role of the "fighter" I hated fighting because I had always been a gentle loving person. I was supposed to be bubbly little Cece singing and dancing to my own drum. I was suspended at least 3 times during middle school and no matter how big and bad I thought I was I lost every single fight. My mother would high five me and tell me good job for standing up to bullies, but I somehow felt ashamed and guilty. I was no longer her perfect child, but she saw me…My role as the fighter got a standing ovation but I didn't like how it felt deep down. 8th grade is where I started dating a guy I was so happy because I felt that someone finally saw me. We were not allowed to date so I never told anyone except my close friends. When I found out that he was dating another girl I was heartbroken but who could I tell and whose shoulder could I cry on I wasn't allowed to date. My secret boyfriend left me with a secret heartbreak. Eventually, my sister found out and snitched to my parents. I continuously struggled throughout school the whole year and I never realized why I couldn't focus. My grades slipped and my mother was quick to remind me of her expectations. I was determined that I would focus on my grades. She would always say things like "remember the 7 B's Books Before Boys Because Boys Bring Babies" I knew I needed to do better so that she wouldn't be disappointed in me. I had to show her that I was good enough. From then on, I begin to play a different role…I tried to stay focused on good grades. Not for myself and not for my future but because my mother said so. The studious one.

"The privilege of a lifetime is to become who you truly are."

— Carl Gustav Jung

CHAPTER 4

The Studious One and The Rebellious One

Being the creative one out of the bunch I wanted to be the jack of all trades. I was good at being innovative. I would write, draw and design and perform in theatrical productions. I knew in my early years of high school the path I wanted to take in life. All I had to do was keep my grades high, stay involved in extracurricular activities and prove to those around me that I could be successful. I started to realize that mathematics was a struggle for me and no matter how hard I studied my parents were always told that I was an "average" student. My younger sister got phenomenal grades and was invited into all the special programs and societies and a lot of times it seemed to be with little effort if any. I hid further in the shadows because now I had an older sister, a senior and more popular and was involved in all the extracurriculars and a younger sister who everyone recognized for her grades. Some may say this sounds like jealousy, yet I applauded them and supported them through every accomplishment. However, living in the shadows of my sisters caused me to long for the attention from others. I began to morph and shape-shift when I got around different groups of people to fit in but what I failed to understand the more I tried to fit in, the less I was seen. Growing up in a household with a strong black mother, there was very little room for children making decisions for themselves. We ate what was made or nothing at all, the clothes and shoes we wore were barely what we chose unless it fit within the budget of school clothes that year. There was no choice in who I took to prom my senior year and little room to choose even what I wanted to wear.

My relationship with my mother began to waver because my true thoughts and feelings could not be spoken so I started to suppress a lot of feelings. I told myself that no matter what I did or no matter how many accomplishments I got or performances I did it was never enough. It triggered anxiety and rage and this caused me to fall into a deep state of depression. I was constantly overstimulated, and my mood never seemed to be balanced. I began to think something was wrong with me. I questioned if I was enough and If I was loved and I second guessed and criticized every little thing about myself. I felt like I had no voice. I always felt deeply misunderstood and our parents set very high expectations for us that sometimes felt like it was too far to reach. My mother and I would fight and argue if I spoke up about a boy I liked that she didn't approve of or talked about a dress that I liked that she didn't like or talked about going away to a college that was too far away. These things may seem like they are shallow, but deeper within they were only a symptom of deeper-rooted issues that have been festering. Old trauma and years of old wounds that were still open and even though I love my mother I still felt such anger towards her. Not because I couldn't date who I wanted or she didn't like the same dress I liked or because of the college she thought I should attend, but in those moments, I didn't feel like anything I ever was or did was ever good enough for her. I felt like I couldn't be my raw and true self. I couldn't speak my truth, and I feared that she was holding me back from living my dreams. I would sit in my room and cry to God because I didn't understand my purpose. Why would God bring me here for me to be silent and invisible? I was never shy because I wanted people to see me. Growing up in church my youth pastor would always say "why try to fit in when you are made to stand out?" I never really understood what that meant but I did everything I could to stand out. I started auditioning for more plays, I tried out for sports, was the vice president of my class, even tried being homecoming queen and still, no one saw me. I still felt invisible and alone. By my junior year I was finally really able to date. Although I was talking to guys the whole 9th and 10th grade year. I had my eyes set on my own crush, but my mother had her own vision of who I should spend my last years of high school with. I introduced her to a close friend of mine, and I knew that he had a crush on me. However, I was quick to put him in the friend zone. He asked me to go to the Friday night football game with him and my mom insisted that I went. So, finally I said okay, and I couldn't enjoy myself. He was weird and clingy and possessive. Anyone that knows me knows that I'm the type that needs space and I don't do well with overly clingy people. He was tall and lanky with thick glasses and watched Anime and spent all 4 years of high school in the ROTC program. To a semi-popular 17-year-old trying to run for homecoming queen and student government it was not my cup of tea but, to gain the approval of my mother, I tried to give him a chance. The next couple of weeks he followed me to and from class. If another guy spoke to me he would get jealous He would get angry. If I chose not to sit with him during lunch and he would be waiting at my locker at the end of the day. I know this all seems sweet to some and some of you may say I should have been grateful to have a guy like that in high school, but something wasn't right, and I sensed it. I ended the relationship that probably lasted about 3 weeks. I wrote a note and slipped it in his locker, and it was the first time where I had to have a hard conversation and break someone else's heart. Later that day after he received the note he was in tears. He walked into our art class, and he became so angry when he saw me that he punched the wall. I had never seen him become violent or even hurt anyone. A shadow of guilt came over me and that day and I learned deep down in my subconscious mind that if I told anyone the truth, it would hurt them. By the end of my senior year, I had applied to a number of different art schools. I was focusing on enjoying my last year of high school. My grades were up. I had a 3.5 gpa. I knew that this was going to be my year. I was more than semi-popular. I had been voted vice president of my class and I was treasurer of the art club. I was driving myself to school in my parents' minivan of course and other than the occasional soccer mom in the minivan joke, life was great. I was preparing for the prom, and I was nervous only because I knew that If my mother didn't approve of my date or my dress we would turn into a screaming match. I hated fighting with her. My mother and I would get into physical altercations because I never took the time to understand her pain and I never even spoke about mine. She would get so angry and lash out and I would have to defend my mental and physical self because I was already broken enough. I felt unloved and unsupported and what I failed to realize is that my mother's way of showing love to her children was by protecting them. She had told us stories of how she grew up and we even saw a lot of her and my grandmother's struggle's firsthand and she tried her best to create a better life than what she was given. When it was time for the prom, she didn't approve of the guy chose neither did she approve of my dress. The guy I was actually interested in she never met so she didn't know anything about him and my dress was too expensive. The other dress choices had too many ruffles or too many sequins or didn't fit the way she wanted. So, I compromised and got something that was on clearance and that she approved of. The guy that I took to prom went to our church and he was a freshman attending another school in another district. We were friends but not best friends. I'm not going to sit up and say that I didn't have fun on my prom night, yet in that moment I was angry and to save myself from a huge argument or worse not being able to go to prom at all I sucked it up and put a smile on and attempted to make the best of it. I was angry and Mentally, I had my hands tied behind my back and duct tape was over my mouth. I would cry at night, but I didn't want anyone to hear me because if I ripped the duct tape off my mouth about my feelings, my anger, my struggles it would be conflict. It wasn't until I got older that I realized that the more that I vowed to not be like my mother, the more I would have to walk out those judgements someday. Often we hear the scripture, judge not lest you be judged but this doesn't only mean verbal judgements that we make towards others, but it also means internal thoughts that we have towards others. Saying things like " I would never do something like that" or "When I grow up, I'm going to make sure that my kids never lack anything." When the fact is we don't know what people are dealing with internally or what circumstances are affecting their daily lives. I've always been somewhat of an empath, but I lacked empathy for those that I felt had hurt me or harmed me in some way. I didn't have any empathy for my father that abandoned me, and I never understood my mother's perspective. Her trauma taught me to be fearful of what others may feel or say. It also taught me that there is a lot of evil in the world, and no one is going to care for you like your mom can. I lived my whole life in fear and silence because I wanted to please people and along with me being an empath the anxiety of me wanting to do right by others and make them happy seemed to overwhelm me. If things were not perfect and I felt as if someone was going to judge or criticize me I would be anxious and I felt as if the world would fall from up under me. So, imagine a dreamer with big dreams but constantly living in a toxic cycle of trying to achieve perfection and comparing myself to others. I wanted to travel the world doing all the things that people said I couldn't do. Partly because I loved doing those things but also to prove a point to show that I can achieve what they said I couldn't. Close to me graduating high school I applied to a few different schools with mostly art programs. Some out of state. I had my mind set that I was going to be an art major and graduate with a cool job as an executive designer and travel the world. I applied to an art school in Atlanta and was accepted. We went to tour the school and from then I was ready to take the world by storm. Only to realize that the cost of out-of-state tuition and the fact that there were no dorms on campus threw a wrench in my plans for my life. I was 18 years old with an ego and I never really did well with people trying to convince me to change my mind when I've had it made up. I had to compromise and humble myself and see things from my parents perspective. They had six children, four girls that were either almost in college or starting college and along with that my parents felt as if I was not ready to live in a huge city on my own starting a new life at 18. Some may say well you're grown at 18 so why not just move? Right? Let's put things into perspective. Growing up in a small town, the fear of the world was all you knew aligned with my mother's fears of past trauma resurfacing only deepened that fear. She was not ready to let me go into a world that she thought to be cold, dark and evil. She thought the worst-case scenario and projected that fear so much that it controlled every decision that I made. I felt that without her approval my life wouldn't amount to anything. So, I settled, I was however grateful that I was able to attend a summer summit program at the school after my 11th grade year. Yet, I still ended up compromising and put what I wanted at the time on pause. I resented my mother and again suppressed my feelings and thoughts and got accepted to The University of South Carolina Upstate as a Bachelor of Arts major in graphic design. The school was 45 minutes away from my hometown, I had no job, no car and I just bought my own first prepaid cell phone with what I saved from working at McDonalds and the local grocery store in high school. To be completely honest I didn't care about any of that. I was just ready to get away from my mother. Starting my freshman year on campus away from home I made a few friends and even had a boyfriend on campus. I had every intention of trying my hardest to graduate and make my mom proud. I had 3 scholarships. The SC Life Scholarship, The SC hope scholarship and the other was a $1,000 scholarship through Walmart. The rest of my tuition room and books was through student loans and I remember that I owed $1,600 and I thought that I was not going to be able to start classes that year and a friend that I met on campus called her father and he wrote a check for $1,600 without question. I had never met her father a day in my life, but I was grateful but deep down I was not happy. I never told my parents that someone covered my remaining tuition. I didn't want them to be upset that I had taken money from someone that I didn't know. My mother didn't know very much about being on a college campus. She had 2 children by the age of 19 and she went to community college to get her first degree. She never lived on campus in a dorm or experienced the prepaid college meal plans or had the opportunity to participate in campus activities. I didn't understand her perspective at that time. She was proud that I was accepted and wanted to help me have the best experience that I could possibly have. Our relationship seemed to improve. I remember that I was given money from all of our family and friends for high school graduation. She took me shopping and let me choose what I wanted for my dorm. I was so excited and happy that we finally had a moment where we can bond and be happy together with no drama. No fights or arguments. Just us. She helped me set up my dorm and I remember her crying because little Cece was no longer little Cece. I couldn't see how she was proud that I had walked a different path than what she chose, and I couldn't see that her whole mission was to create a better life for her children. I was just angry and rebellious, and I didn't recognize the root of my rage. My mission quickly turned from making mamma proud to making myself happy. I rebelled and started losing focus on the things that were really important. I tried studying but never really could stay focused, but the work got harder, the lectures got longer, and I felt like I couldn't succeed. In high school I had to study a little here and there but in college I had to study and work ten times harder. It seemed like all the other students seemed to pick up on information and retain it easily. I would study and not be able to sit through a study session. I would get to class, take an exam and fail the exams. I started comparing myself to everyone else around me. I felt like something was wrong with me. I questioned myself constantly and started to wonder if in high school I only failed one class and that was 10th grade geometry. I started skipping class because all I wanted to do was sleep. I complained and constantly had a negative mindset. I began to party and hang out late to mask the pain that I felt. I never knew that my reckless behavior was a sign of depression and anxiety. My GPA quickly dropped, and I didn't seem to care. Everyone around knew me as the life of the party, quirky, with an outgoing personality but they didn't know me enough to know that something was wrong. I had tons of "friends" that were alongside me supporting me in my mess, but no one kept it real. By second semester, I changed my major to Performing Arts theatrical studies. I was excited that this would be an opportunity for a new beginning and a new start. I would be able to do something that mattered to me. I auditioned for plays on campus and I was excited to tell my family about what I was doing...

Changing my major was the first "adult" decision that I made for myself, but I forgot one little detail. Did my mother approve of this? I felt anxiety and finally built up the courage to call her and tell her what I did. Things went further downhill after that. I had gotten the role in a musical on campus "Urinetown" the rehearsals went weeknights and weekends and even holidays. I remember it being Good Friday and we didn't have class that day, but we had play rehearsals. My mother's plans for me that weekend was to come home and spend the Easter weekend with family. That was not my plan. In my eyes I was an adult, and I could make my own decisions. My mother quickly reminded me that I wasn't. I remember she showed up and found her way to my rehearsal and said that I was coming home. I understand it was Easter weekend, but I wanted to make decisions and live my life on my own terms. She sat and waited until I got out of rehearsal and drove me back to my dorm and packed my bag for the weekend so that I would come home. After trying to speak about my wants, I settled and compromised and said okay. Deep down I was furious, and I continued to suppress the rage. I felt like all she wanted to do was control me and control my life, control who I talked to and where I went, what I wore, the way I walked, talked and breathed. After going back to campus, I didn't call my mother for weeks. I used the excuse that I didn't have any minutes on my prepaid cell phone but there were other phones around campus that I could have used. By the end of freshman year, I was offered a RA position on campus. I was shocked because quite frankly I didn't think I deserved it. There were strict requirements, No disciplinary refractions from the university, I must be enrolled full time, and a minimum gpa requirement of 3.0 This would be an opportunity for my housing to be completely covered for as long as I have the position. I couldn't wait to tell my family about the offer, and it would save them money for the next three years of my college career. I would be in charge of planning all freshman activities for my dorm and when I told my mother about this she was excited to hear. Aside from my high school graduation, it was one of the few times where I actually felt she was proud of me. I began to thrive within my newfound major studying theater and things started looking up. Except one more little detail I didn't disclose. My GPA had dropped to a 2.9. My first semester habits had caught up with me and I felt like a complete failure. I lost the opportunity to be an RA and once again I was back home in my parents' home and things began to go further downhill.

Back home, I ended up enrolling at Piedmont Technical College and would drive to and from class in my parents vehicle every day. I needed my own car, so I decided to start working again. I got my job back a job at the local grocery store and I struggled saving money because I loved to spend and shop. I was 19 years old and still driving my parents' minivan to my college classes every day. I felt like life was moving slowly and all I knew was my small town down in Laurens County. While I was at Piedmont Tech I met a guy and deep down I knew he was not good for me. He was what we would consider a hood nigga. Everything that he did my parents taught me not to do growing up and I was intrigued. One day I decided not to go to class, and we met up at his house. After sleeping with him I came back outside, and the battery was dead in my parents' minivan. I knew that I had a great aunt and an older cousin that lived around the corner. If my parents found out that I was with this guy instead of in class, it would be over! I finally buckled down and called my aunt's house and asked to speak to my cousin. Forgetting how nosey my aunt was I discreetly told my cousin what happened. When I got back home that day, my mom asked me what I was doing over on the other side of Laurens when my classes were only 15 minutes away. She was livid. I can laugh about this story today but back then she was ready to put me out and I didn't quite mind it either. My dad took me to go searching for apartments and I got a job with the disabilities and special needs to help cover rent. I chose an apartment that was a studio apartment in a decent neighborhood but there was black mold all in the walls. My dad warned me about the concerns he had but I was not trying to listen to that. I was still trying to save money for a car. My rent was $350.00 a month and I purchased my own groceries my own cell phone plan and my light bill was over $400.00 a month. If you ever lived in Clinton, South Carolina then you know how that goes. I walked to and from work on some days and caught rides with my friends sometimes. If I needed food I would walk to the grocery store. I was determined not to ask my parents for anything unless absolutely necessary. I struggled so much but my pride was so big that I would rather suffocate in that moldy apartment than to go running back. I started partying more with my friends and cousins and I would ride up to Greenville to hit the nightclubs every weekend. Partying, drinking and even on the coldest days of winter we'd stand out waiting in line with the shortest dresses and stilettos to get in free before eleven. Even more so, I was living the life, Well at least I thought I was. The thought of finding someone who I thought could truly love me outweighed the thought of catching pneumonia in the dead of winter. Partying and alcohol seemed to fill the void of validation. Alcohol brought out another side of me, I was wild, confident, free yet dark, impulsive, provocative and promiscuous. I was broken but I refused to let others around me see my weakness. Little did I know, my perfect porcelain mask was starting to crack, and it was getting harder to hide my true self. Up under the mask I was alone, afraid, empty, lost and I had no one I could talk to.

Chapter 5

The Vixen and The Fighter

Broken, I found myself going from relationship to relationship.Searching for someone to fill my voids. All I wanted was someone to see that I was worthy enough to be loved and valued for who I was. So, I put on the mask of "The Promiscuous One" or let's just say, "The Vixen". I gave my body, my mind and opened my spirit to men who left me even more broken and empty after fulfilling their lustful desires. Trying to prove with my body that I was worthy of their love, sex became my drug. I was addicted to the sensations that my body felt and the dopamine that was released in my brain and soon I began bringing home partners from the night clubs and meeting guys online to get my fix. Although I was all in with the choices I made I always seemed to feel violated and disgusting while I was in the act. But my soul was in too deep, and I could no longer hear the convictions that were instilled in me as a child. I would get overly drunk to get through those nights and when those highs would come down and I would be right back to feeling empty. I would beat myself up and I thought of myself as a hoe, dirty, freak and to numb those feelings I would turn around and do it all over again. Deep down all I wanted was the "relationship goals" that I saw on Facebook. I was completely delusional comparing myself to other girls who I thought were better than me. I was competing in a contest that didn't exist.

I was 20 years old when I met him. He was a few years older than me at the time and I was completely infatuated. He was one that your parents warned you about. The one that all the good girls go after, the bad boy. We met at a club one night and I was playing hard to get. We eventually exchanged phone numbers, and we began talking regularly. He started coming to stay the night in my apartment on weekends when he was off from school and quickly began to see red flags. He was quick to anger. He would get into fights in the clubs. There would be times when we would argue and he would call me out of my name and degrade me, embarrass me in front of our friends, and would even "pretend to hit me " just to see how far I would let him go. We had a long-distance relationship so I would find ways to go see him and pick him up even with no car. I knew that this was not right, but I thought that if I loved him enough then he would change. Although we were different in many ways we were both broken, empty and angry. We both had red flags and neither of us ever stopped to address them. I was lying to myself telling myself that I could change him but all along I had my own red flags that I needed to address. One night we got into a huge argument because he said that I was cheating on him. We were laying in my bed and arguing, and he was calling me names using profound language.I was triggered and irate and I told him to get out of my bed. He refused to move so I pushed him onto the floor and demanded that he leave my apartment. I proceeded to walk towards the front door to throw his things out and he pushed me up against the wall with his hands around my throat and I was fighting to breathe. After he let me go, I remember taking a lamp from the living room table and throwing it at him, hitting him in the head. I began thinking back on the vows that I made to myself that I wouldn't end up getting beaten like my mother and grandmother. I was afraid for my life as he grabbed me by my face and mushed my head into the wall and locking my jaw. I was in a rage, and I remember holding a knife in my hand and I threatened to kill him. That night was the darkest night of my life. I couldn't call the police because I was afraid that I too would go to jail. He told me that if I told my parents or family or friends about the fight then they would put us in jail. I kept it a secret only telling my closest friends. The next day my mother came to pick me up and asked what happened to my face. There were scratches and bruises left under my eye and my jawline. I smiled and attempted to put on a mask and said "Oh I don't know how that happened, it's fine though" but my mask began to crack, and my eyes became heavy with tears . I was silent the whole ride and tears streamed down my face. He apologized and promised to never hurt me again…

That night my first daughter was conceived. I cried; I was shattered to pieces. Yet I was still delusional enough to love someone who had shown me so many times before that he didn't love me the way that I should be loved.

Chapter 6

The Perfect Mother

I was 21 years old finding out I was pregnant, and I knew I wasn't ready for motherhood. I cried because how could I love a child when I didn't even love myself? It took me a couple of weeks to break the news hoping that this would make things better between us. I remember texting him and his only response was " Nah, can't be me…Who else you been F***ing!?" The thing is he knew about my past because I confided in him about my previous relationships. He chose to weaponize them against me. I went through the majority of the first and second trimester alone because I taught myself to try to figure things out on my own. I was in survival mode and hid myself away from the world . I no longer wanted to be seen or heard or felt. I just wanted true love, unconditional love. I attempted to move on and move forward but I just felt hurt, guilty and ashamed. I was in the darkest place in my life, and I remember him telling me that I should just get rid of the baby. It's interesting how things come back around because that's the same thing that my grandmother told my mom when she was pregnant with me. I became guarded and I hid her from those who wanted to hurt her. I eventually moved back home with my parents in Mauldin, South Carolina. December 17, 2010, I finally gave birth to my beautiful baby girl. I was lost but I found hope and joy in giving birth to my daughter. Finally, I had someone who could love me unconditionally. I wanted to be perfect for her. When she was born nothing else in the world mattered to me, but I was deeply afraid. I didn't know who else I could turn to or depend on. My mother and I began working on our relationship, but we were still strained. At the age of 21 had moved out and lived a life on my own terms but failed. I was afraid so I trusted her judgment when it came to motherhood. Even though we had struggles she was still an amazing mother. I knew she would protect me and my daughter with her life. I knew deep down she loved me and was passionate about her children. Yet, I still wanted to live my life as an adult. There was a power struggle because although by then I was an adult with my own child, I was still humbled and put back in a child's place. If I decided that I felt was best for me and she didn't agree it would cause an argument or a physical altercation. Sometimes, the decisions I made were pure foolery but other times they were legitimate decisions that were in good intention for my daughter and me . The truth is I was still young trying to navigate motherhood, my life and finding out who I was. I remember my parents talking to me two weeks after getting home from giving birth and my mother telling me that when I was younger I was sexually violated as a child by a family member.I was about three or four years old and as she was telling me tears immediately started pouring down my face. She told me that while my great grandmother was looking after me while my mom was working my older cousin touched me , violated me and exposed me to things that I shouldn't have experienced as a child. My mind quickly shifted back to my dreams that I had as a child and teenager where I was hiding under the table at my great grandmother's house. I was shocked because my whole life I thought that those nightmares were just a figment of my imagination. My mother never told me these things happened to me until after I gave birth to my daughter. Yet somehow I remembered exactly what she was talking about because everything she told me aligned directly with the nightmares I had. I was disappointed that she never told me, but I still had grace for her because I already knew the kind of life that she had as a child. I knew that she did everything in her power to protect me in those times. She didn't want me living the life she lived, nor did she want me to walk out the trauma and the generational curses that her, her sister and my grandmother had to endure. I carried around that vile spirit my whole childhood and never understood why I felt inferiority and why I hated myself so much and even why I made certain impulsive decisions with my sexuality. My parents prayed with me that day that the soul ties would be broken from my life. I had learned from church growing up that he in pure was the way of God and anytime there were sexual encounters with someone there was a soul exchange that took place and part of your soul would be tied to the other person. That only made me feel more guilty because I knew that I had many soul ties before. However, I just suppressed the feelings as usual and just moved on. I didn't feel anything different that day. I was living a double life. I continued to live a reckless life full of lust, drinking and partying. I went back to being a vixen jumping from relationship to relationship and bed to bed and self-medicating with alcohol to avoid the feelings that I suppressed. Still desperate for love, I tried to work things out with my daughter's father AGAIN. Only this time it resulted in more toxicity; more disappointment and my daughter were in the middle of all of it. The lie was I was over the hurt and disappointment and the delusion was that I could trust that he wouldn't hurt me or my child…I let the guilt of my daughter growing up without her father in her life make me make the emotional decision to allow him to come back around. I finally opened up and talked to my mom about what I had decided and at that moment my whole world was turned upside down. Things went from zero to one hundred and I never realized that one little decision would cause such a physical altercation between my whole family and me. My mother and I got into a fight which led to my father coming to her defense. By then my brothers were in high school and also living at home and they came to diffuse the situation without question. By then, we were all fighting, throwing things at each other and I was enraged because I never understood what I did wrong other than attempt to make a decision that I felt was best for my daughter at the time. I remember being put out on the curb with my daughter and a bag of clothes. My younger sister had been at work and she was my only means of transportation but I had no car of my own and no way to get away from the trauma that I experienced. I was desperate and I called the one whom I despised the most. My daughter's father. I couldn't understand why things turned so far left so I went the total opposite way that I was told not to go. We eventually got back together and   attempted to work things out but it was worse because by then I was poison.. I became everything I hated about him. I became a narcissist, manipulative, deceptive and I could care less about anyone else but myself and my daughter. I became a fighter again moving around the same mountains that I've hiked many times before. I failed to see the successful things that were going on in my life. I was attending college completing my first associates degree, moved into my second apartment with my sister and was raising my daughter and I told myself that it was all good. Yet the truth was I wasn't the perfect mother but I did my best, the lie I told myself was I was a horrible mother and the delusion was I was "just being myself" I became the party girl for my friends the vixen, the lover, the prideful one and in front of family, I became the "holier than thou" church girl".

Chapter 7

The "Holier Than Thou" Church Girl

After 2 years of my sister and I living in our apartment, she moved away to Columbia and I moved back home for the second time. I was trying my best to be what I thought my family thought I should be. I was going to church working in the children's ministry, I was working full time, about to graduate school. I finally somewhat had a car, and as long as I didn't have an opinion and I did everything that I was told and taught to do there was no conflict. I was hidden and shrunk myself down and stayed silent to not take up any space. It had been 3 years since I had my daughter and in November of 2014 I met my husband. We were both attending the same college, and he saw me in the computer lab. Instead of working and completing all my assignments I was casually talking to a group of friends about movies and overheard 2 other students talking about the movie I wanted to see … "The Best Man Holiday" I intervened and said, "I want to see that movie too!" One of our classmates jokingly told this guy "Man you should take your sister!" We all laughed and by the end of the night after class one of the guys approached me saying, "My buddy wanted me to give you his number" I looked around confused because I didn't see anyone else around. Quite frankly I was ready to grow up and I wasn't thinking about a relationship. I was dealing with a mess and drama with my daughter's father. I had just gotten out of a 2-year failed long distance relationship, yet I took a chance and went looking for him. By the time I got to the parking lot he was gone. The next day, I texted him and we became friends. A few days later we went on our first date, and we saw "The Best Man Holiday" . I studied him and I noticed how different he was. He was quiet, calm and calculated. He was very observant and although he was not big on words, he had an amazing smile that would light up a room. He was intelligent yet he had this mystery about him. We would laugh at the silliest things together and we seemed to fit fairly well together. I felt so comfortable around him. I felt a peace that I had never felt in any other relationship. We began going out regularly and he was a gentleman. We eventually became sexually involved and we were officially exclusive. My parents loved him, and he would come to family functions, and he even grew closely attached to my daughter. I let my guard down and I trusted him. When I had to work long hours, and my parents couldn't babysit he stepped in and asked his family to help, and they did. His family became my family and my family became his. We were in a place where we became very serious after about 6 and a half months. We decided to attend each other's churches. I was attending a mega church in Greenville, South Carolina and he was still attending his small family church in Hodges, South Carolina. By then I had not been to a traditional church since my parents first got married back in 1995. The people were nice, but I wasn't happy there. I felt restricted to wear traditional church clothes. We sang songs that were traditional and out-dated. There was no dance ministry, no lights, no cameras and I questioned why he still attended. The pastor had a familiar spirit, one that I had seen before. It wasn't the same man, but I could smell the toxicity long before I became a member. I still would visit regularly because I knew it made my then boyfriend happy and his family accepted me. In May 2014 we found out that I was expecting my second child. I was shocked that I was pregnant but even more so, I was overwhelmed with fear and anxiety from my previous traumas. Our relationship was far from perfect, but I felt safe knowing that he wouldn't physically hurt me. He was sick from the fear of being a father and even more so the weight of the pressure of having another child out of wedlock became overbearing. I knew that I didn't want another child growing up in a broken home. I was tired of being a single mother. Both of our families were very religious, so we were taught the consequences of having children out of the bounds of marriage. He was forced to move out of his parents' home and within a short period of time moved into our first apartment together. Everyone wanted to give us advice and their opinions on how we should handle the situation. We were told that "We should do right by God" "God is not pleased" and "Ya'll are shacking up and living in sin!" For those of you who may not understand the relevance of all this, growing up a young black woman in the south "The Bible Belt" we are taught maintaining your abstinence and your virginity makes you pure, undefiled, clean and it brings you closer to God…well based on the previous chapters I was far from that. Yes, was still attending church and serving in the ministry but even more so I always question as a child if I had been violated what does that say to me or any other woman that had been taken advantage of assaulted, or raped? What does that tell the little girl that is being molested by her stepfather, uncle or cousin? What about the young teenager who is being groomed by their neighborhood predator or someone they trust? So maybe you can understand why I was angry at myself. I also knew the feeling of growing up in a home with a single mother and I didn't want my children to continue the cycles of a broken home. I was told that it's always good to be with someone through every

season of their lives to see who they truly are. All I knew is that I was in love, and I felt safe and comfortable with him. He was a gentle soul, quiet and introverted, and educated. He was younger than I and grew up in a sheltered home. I knew I wanted to be married, and I felt like I was ready in spite of all the trauma that was hidden beneath the surface. In December 2014 we graduated from college at the same time. I remember having a huge stomach and embarrassed that I was pregnant at graduation, and I was only getting an associate's degree. I felt like life should have been further along. I should have gotten a bachelor's degree by now and I should be married by buying my first home. As time went by, and seasons changed I began to see different sides of him that I was not okay with yet were left unspoken. In February 2015 I gave birth to my second born. This was one of the proudest moments of my life along with having my first born. We had discussed getting married and I was overjoyed but deep down I questioned if it was the right timing and was he the one? We were not in the best place financially. He proposed in April of 2015.
During the time of our engagement, he had lost 2 jobs and was grieving the loss of his grandmother, and our daughter was just born. He eventually got a job through a temp agency working nights, but things got worse. He became distant and even more quiet, and I noticed that the communication became short, cold, blunt and sometimes nonexistent. I pretty soon began to feel less

acknowledged, less validated and heard even when I attempted to include myself in his world and in his space I was pushed away and shut out. I was overworked, overwhelmed and overstimulated and I had very little help with the household or the kids. My mental, physical and psychological needs were dismissed and neglected and while fighting my own demons and dealing postpartum depression, I was afraid, and I began having suicidal and homicidal thoughts. It got so bad that I wouldn't trust myself staying at home alone at night. I would go stay the night at my parents just to avoid dealing with the chaos that was going on in my own home. I feared that I would hurt myself and my children. Just about every night I cried and prayed that the pain would be taken away from me. Pain I couldn't even describe or even knew what it meant. All I knew is I was hurting deep like something dark and viral was on the inside of me festering and eating me alive. I didn't want to live life anymore and felt hopeless. I told him how I felt and no matter how much I expressed my concerns he didn't hear me. I became even better with covering my emotions and hiding my expressions and my feelings because I couldn't go to church showing how broken I was singing and leading worship. I couldn't express to my parents that I was unhappy and miserable, and I couldn't express that I didn't like how I was treated because I was always taught to never speak down on your husband or defile your marriage. Also, I wanted so badly to have someone close to me that I could say was mine and loved me unconditionally. I thought I could change him and fix him into loving me the way that I wanted him to love me. I again became invisible. I wanted to be seen, heard and validated. I quickly realized that I wanted to use my gifts and talents to help the ministry grow. Yet, I was acting in vain out of my own selfish motives. I volunteered to sing on the praise team. On the outside looking in, life seemed so simple. We go to work, come home, go to church, pay bills and do it all over again. I felt stuck in a rut but every day that we let slide by without dealing with our mess the more we hoarded the more it festered. I knew there was more to life than what we were living, and I knew that I was tired of carrying the weight of my trauma, but I was afraid to face my demons and the fear of it all seemed to overwhelm me even more.

Chapter 8

The Perfect Wife and the Holier Than Thou Church Girl

July 11, 2015, we were married. It wasn't the most glamorous wedding as I dreamt of as a child, but I settled and compromised because we only had four months to plan but I thought this would fix all of our problems and everything will be better. We continued attending his church and I was baptized there. Sunday mornings we would put on our perfect family mask and Monday through Saturday we were living in a mess. We were evicted from our apartment and eventually had to move. We were living from paycheck to paycheck and even though we had decent jobs we struggled to make ends meet. We weren't getting along and the more we avoided dealing with the junk the more it festered and piled up. We were good at hiding our issues from each other and from the rest of the world. After living in our new apartment for about 5 years we decided that it was time for us to purchase our first home. We worked together to clear out debt and got over the hump of living paycheck to paycheck. He was no longer working through the temp agency but was hired on full time by the company. This was a major accomplishment that we both were proud of, and we thought that somehow a new home would make things better. The truth is a new house, and a new job doesn't fix internal things. We were just masking our mess with materialistic things. I had taken a job at a local charter school and things were starting to look up for us. Except, everything wasn't all flowers and rainbows. I grew more and more weary with church. The environment became more toxic and when it came time to go I would feel physically ill. I'd started therapy for the first time, and I thought that it was me who had all the problems. I started pointing out things that didn't necessarily sit well such as public embarrassment from the pulpit, gossip, disrespectful, and snarky jokes, and other passive aggressive behavior. We were corrected and spoken to as if we were children if we missed service or decided that we wouldn't attend. We would even get called out about what we wore if it wasn't deemed "pleasant to God". Ironically, the more I hated it the more I started to conform to it. I was so used to putting on that mask every Sunday morning, and Wednesday nights, that I lost who I was and became that same judgmental, religious person that I hated. This part of the book has been the hardest to write thus far because this is where life started to shift for me, and I began to realize that I had lost myself. I looked in the mirror and didn't know who I was, and I didn't understand my purpose. I lost sight of my goals and aspirations. All I knew was, I was tired. I was tired of carrying the weight of everyone else's world on my shoulders. I was tired of being triggered. I was tired of masking my trauma. I was tired of pretending everything was okay, but I couldn't show anyone including my family the broken places. Not even realizing that the ones closest to me saw right through me. I knew I was broken but I kept going through the motions. Singing in church every Sunday, ministering on the praise dance team, but on the inside all hell was breaking loose.

In 2016, I reconnected with an old friend that I worked with. She and I connected quickly. I had other best friends, but she and I were unbreakable, so we thought around that time, I also found love in acting again and landed my first debut acting gig in 2018. I realized that I was better at it than I thought. I begin to see all of the standing ovations and awards I got from performing on stage. I got high off the validation that I received from the world. It was a childhood need that I lacked and yearned for even 29 years later. Acting was an outlet for me. I realized that I found purpose in acting but then I never realized that it wasn't for me but for others. I began to participate more and more in these stage plays and ironically I was doing exactly what I was doing my whole life...playing charades, pretending but acting seemed to be an escape from the soap opera in my own life. I looked to my best friend for support in what I was trying to accomplish in my dreams. I realized that she would decline the invitations, and I thought maybe this was not her thing or maybe she didn't have the resources to come but I was very observant in how things never worked out when it was time for a show. I let it all roll off my back because I noticed that I was finding joy again in acting. Yet it seemed like in the brightest times of my life there would be a dark cloud somewhere lurking around the corner. Even finding a healthy stress outlet and time for myself, seemed to bring a wedge in my marriage. My husband felt neglected when I would be in rehearsals on long nights and tech rehearsals for days at a time. He even felt insecure about the romance roles that I had to portray. There was a time where he even asked if I could quit acting for a while to focus on him. I began to second guess if this was what I was supposed to be doing. Was I neglectful to him and my children? I realized that I had not done anything for myself since being married aside from the occasional manicure or buying myself clothes or allowing myself a night out with friends. Those things didn't define me, and they surely didn't bring me joy and genuine happiness. No matter if I forgot my lines on stage or fell on my face, my eyes still lit up with genuine peace and joy like a child when I was in my creative element. So, I became more resentful. He became more distant, and we seemed to be many universes apart.

2020 Covid took the world by storm. We had just finished the stage play "A Daughter Scorned" written, produced and directed by my mother and the world was shut down. Church was canceled, I had to work partly from home and some days in the school. I can remember being afraid that I would get sick and my whole world would fall apart. I had just signed with a local talent agency, and I can remember not feeling supported by my husband. My mother and I were working towards bettering our relationship, but I felt like I couldn't open up to her about the issues that were going on in my marriage. I was working full time, taking care of our two girls, managing their e-learning schedules, cooking, cleaning the house and trying to make sure that a roof was over our heads. He was still working the night shift at the time, and I felt like a married single mother. I had no help with the kids, no help cleaning, and I realized that he became more and more distant. After coming home from work there would be no acknowledgement that I was even there waiting on him to come home. He would go upstairs and watch television and fall asleep. I was lonely, our children were at each other's throats and things were falling apart. I got to the point where I would drink a glass of wine or take a shot almost every night just to numb the pain where I didn't even realize the source. I fell deeper and deeper into depression and spent plenty of my nights crying myself to sleep. Listening to sad depressing songs that swept me to sleep. I struggled with insomnia and frequent nightmares and even sometimes fought with sleep paralysis. My insecurities played over and over in my head telling me I wasn't enough, that I had no purpose, that my life was no good. I told myself that I wasn't loved and appreciated by my husband and that he had found someone better. One day I decided to check his phone, and I saw conversations back and forth from another woman. I was completely devastated. I was angry because I gave so many years of my life to someone just so that I could prove that I was worthy of being loved. I became enraged and at that moment I chose to live my life for me. I had no care in the world regarding my marriage. I had not been back to church since getting sick and we left our church that same year because I realized that everything that I had done in the church was because I compromised for him. I also realized that I was beginning to question everything that I was taught regarding religion. I was unlearning everything that I learned as a child. A month later our church was involved with a scandal that went public all-over social media and

I vowed to never step foot in a church again. Some may think that this was a bit extreme, or I was exaggerating but I was tired. Every church I joined since my early childhood days was involved in some sort of scandal and if not a scandal, it was someone in the pulpit that operated out of a spirit of control and manipulation, as a dictator in a cult and a wolf in sheep's clothing instead of a shepherd leading their flock. I am not stating that this is my belief for every church in the world but for the best of my spiritual walk and my healing I never went back to a church other than to support family members. I thought I was "protecting my peace" by shutting people out and putting up walls. I became distant from my family and spent more time out with my friends. My late nights became later and the more I drank the more numb I felt. One night I was scrolling through my social media and my friend's husband messaged me on snapchat. In my vulnerability I began to share with him what I was dealing with my husband. I confided in him and asked if he had heard anything about the particular women that my husband was conversing with. I felt convicted but I was delusional in letting myself believe that nothing further would come of this. Weeks passed and we began having more and more late-night conversations. He talked about how he noticed that I wasn't spoiled and taken care of, and he knew that my husband didn't acknowledge and appreciate me. I felt so guilty because I saw how he spoiled his wife and lavished her with gifts and date nights and showed her off to the world. I would sit and watch and think that I wish I had someone who could do those things for me. I started receiving monetary gifts and we would meet up to spend time together. I would start deleting text messages and call logs to hide the fact that we were talking. Although I knew deep down it was not right, eventually we got to the point where we were intimate. I was so angry with myself not because I was worried about my husband, but I was disappointed because I knew that this would destroy the relationship that I had with my friend at the time. My husband soon found out about the affair. He noticed that I was more distant, and I was staying out more and at home I didn't acknowledge that he was around. I barely spoke to him unless it was necessary because any little issue caused an argument. It was like walking on a landmine, saying the wrong thing or making the wrong step and either one of us would explode. I hated walking up feeling empty and I was enraged every time I looked at him. All I could think about was the hurt that he caused on top of all the trauma I was already dealing with the time that I had let myself go for the first years of our marriage because I expected him to be some magical version of a man that I created in my mind that he didn't have full capability to even be in the first place. I set unrealistic expectations that my husband would be the perfect man for me that I fantasized about . That was another lie that I told myself and I was delusional that everyone should treat me the way that I treat them. My husband should cater to me in my illness as I did in his time of illness and that he should know and understand all the things that my dad did. Even though I knew certain things about the way he grew up and what he was taught I never took it into consideration because I was blinded by anger and rage and resentment. I was selfish and all I wanted was someone to hear me… see me … and feel my pain. My best friend and I were like sisters. Her children were my God children, and my children were hers. To take the blame away from myself I started to point out her character flaws and imperfections. Did I love my best friend? Yes. I was devastated when she found out about 6 months later. Even then it took time for me to understand that I should have taken accountability for the hurt that I caused because I still wanted to point the finger at other people. Even though I didn't initiate the conversations, I still made a poor choice to engage. I was so far gone, and I didn't even realize that I was lost. The truth in all this was no one heard me, everyone saw me and everyone around me felt pain that I caused. The next few months to a year I spent apologizing and getting backlash and feeling the wrath of judgment from my family. My mother was informed about the affair, and she was disappointed and couldn't wrap her head around the fact that I was so heinous in my actions. I never told her about my husband's inappropriate conversations with the other woman until months later because I got tired of trying to defend myself. People were going to think what they wanted to think. I also still felt a gleam of empathy for my husband and for some reason I still wanted to protect his image and not deform his name. I sent apologies and messages to my no longer friend at the time and eventually came to the realization that me trying to make my husband feel and understand the pain that I felt was pointless and when they say two wrongs don't make a right I learned that two wrongs only bring more hell into your life. I was grieving the old person that I was, I was also grieving the friendship that was lost, and I was grieving the expectations of the husband that I thought I should have. I cried because I didn't have a proper appetite for weeks. I remember not wanting to get out of bed or take a shower for days at a time. I didn't care about my appearance and acting was the last thing on my mind. I felt a heaviness and it seemed like a dark cloud just hovered over me. My husband and I started counseling, and things began to start moving forward. Deep down I was still angry and broken and I still put a wall up because even though I acknowledged my wrongs and wanted desperately to make things right, but the sunshine only seemed temporary because no matter how bright the sun shines it seems like there is a thunderstorm around the corner.

Chapter 9

Everything To Everybody

Months passed and we had gone through counseling, and I went through mental turmoil. I hated myself. I attempted to reach out to my friend to apologize. I had come to terms with the fact that we would never be friends again after I told her about the situation, but I was grieving the loss of our relationship. I prepared myself whatever karma was to come my way, and I told myself that anything that ever happened to me I deserved it. The struggle that I always had was the fact that I am an empath. I feel other people's pain and I want to do everything in my power to fix problems. Even though I inflicted pain on someone else, someone who I truly cared for and admired. I hurt for her and my husband but most of all I was angry at myself that I went that low just to have someone love me. I still didn't know who I was and there were a lot of times where I didn't recognize myself, but I did know that my actions were not who I was. The easiest thing for me to do was to point the finger at everyone else. I blamed my husband for texting other women, I blamed my friend for how she treated her husband, and I even tried to say that she was not supportive and even though I didn't approach her husband initially, I still had a choice. I had no morals and during the time of the affair I had no morals. I was toxic without a care of who I hurt because I was bitter, angry and broken. No one could tell me anything at that point in my life because I was intentional. I had given my best years to others because I was searching for love in all the wrong places. I know that sounds cliche' but it was my truth. I was so tired of pouring into other people and I could no longer give other people the best version of me because I was empty. As my husband and I attempted to rekindle things I became more stressed. There was little to no trust between us. I couldn't forgive him, and I really didn't even know if he forgave me. We would sit and talk all night and have hard conversations and I felt like he still didn't see the hurt that I was feeling. We were still afraid to speak our hearts and minds to each other because we were afraid to hurt each other. I had conditioned myself to think that when you tell someone the truth it brings trouble. I didn't know how he would react to me telling him that I didn't want to be married anymore. I was fed up with being lonely, I was fed up with the kids, my physical health was declining, and I didn't know who or where I could go to figure it all out without feeling judged. My mother found out about the affair the same day I told my friend, and she was appalled. She was so upset and was very disappointed in the situation. I was in a horrible state of mind because once again I had failed those who cared about me. I knew what I did was wrong but at that moment in time, I felt it was justified. I never even told her about the text messages between my husband and the other woman until months later because deep down I still wanted to protect him. I was beaten down with judgements from everyone around that knew about the affair and in order to feel understood in that moment, I had to take the cover off. I explained to my mother what happened because her not knowing seemed to draw an even bigger wedge in our relationship but this time she heard me. She felt my pain and was able to understand what I was going through without condoning my actions. Even through all of this, I was still dealing with my own traumas and when I was taking steps to move forward life snatched me right back.

September 2021 I was rushed to the hospital. I was experiencing heavy vaginal bleeding and excruciating pain in my abdomen and sides and back. I had gone to work that day and left early and went home, took medicine and fell asleep. At this time my husband moved to the first shift to have more time at home. When he arrived at home, I woke up and told him I was in pain and needed to go to the ER. When we got there, they ran all the tests they could run including a pregnancy test. The thing is I had no signs or symptoms of pregnancy. I just knew that I was always tired which is common for me being a person with low iron. The doctor came in and told me that I was pregnant, and they ordered an emergency ultrasound. It was an ectopic pregnancy and my right fallopian tube burst. I was hemorrhaging and if I had not made it to the hospital I would not have made it out alive. The doctors ordered an emergency surgery that night to remove the tube and the pregnancy had to be terminated. I was in shock because I was only a few weeks pregnant. My husband and I didn't plan on having any other children and it caught both of us by surprise. I was out of work for about three weeks, but I had to depend on the one person that I was angry at the most. I couldn't walk without his assistance. I couldn't eat without him preparing food for me. He had to bathe me and clothe me, and I didn't like the fact that my independence was stripped away from me. He became more distant and everything he did seemed simply transactional. I felt a cold draft coming from him in his body language and the way he spoke and handled me. I remember one night asking him why he was still here? Why was he doing the things that he was doing and taking care of me after all that we have been through? His response was "because I'm your husband and that's what I'm supposed to do." I couldn't wrap my head around that because at that moment I felt like…"REALLY?" "THAT'S ALL YOU'RE GOING TO SAY?" My brain started running ninety miles an hour. So, did he do those things because he loves me and because he cares, and he is glad that I made it out alive? Does he want to take care of me, or does he just have to take care of me? I never even thought about the fact that I was not the only one dealing with this trauma. Yes, it was my body that felt the agonizing pain and my body that almost bled to death, and I was the one dealing with the hormone changes, but it didn't hurt him any less. His pain and trauma were just as valid as mine. I was so caught up in being angry and broken. I had made up the delusion in my head that if you depend on someone they will let you down. I thought that if I was not in control of things in my life the ball would get dropped. I was so used to taking care of things myself I did not trust my husband with my life or my health. My mother helped me realize that there are things that I expect people to just know because I have been taught certain things. I set expectations so high that sometimes he felt like he wasn't able to reach them. I was such a perfectionist that I made him feel like nothing was right. I was always so angry because I would tell him things that I wanted and needed, and it wouldn't happen, or I would open up about my feelings and the conversations would go nowhere. Our whole marriage I was afraid to speak up because I was trying to be his peace. I wanted to make things better for our marriage, be a great mom to our kids, a good sister, a great actor, a teacher, the perfect daughter, a good friend Trying to be everything to everybody, and I thought I would never drop the ball. I was carrying all of my baggage and trauma, trying to break generational curses and fighting physical and mental health issues but I couldn't carry the weight of it all anymore. I recovered from my surgery, and I slowly tried to build that trust again in my marriage. I was still guarded, and we were still going through therapy. My mental health was still in shambles, but I knew I had to get some help. I had always dealt with anxiety, but this was time it was getting more extreme.

September 2023 another health crisis struck. I had stopped teaching because everything became too overwhelming. I was fed up with everyone and everything. I would cry almost every day in my classroom, and I realized that I began to inflict my frustrations on my students and my own children at home. I started to see some of the same patterns happening in my marriage. We weren't speaking, we didn't plan time together and date nights anymore. We were just going through the motions. I knew that we were getting comfortable again and I refused to go back around the same mountain. Only this time I decided to speak up and express my sentiments. I was helping family members with their lives and children, I had attempted to take more college courses again to get my degree back on track trying to follow my mother's footsteps, I was also still acting, I had written and released my first book, and I was trying to juggle it all by myself. I asked my husband to help carry some of the load and things didn't change. One night after work we were all in the living room and trying to enjoy a little family time. I had experienced twitching in my left eye for two months straight and I just assumed that I was extremely tired from lack of sleep and working on computers all day. While sitting on the couch I started to experience a spinning sensation in the room and my whole body went limp. I couldn't speak or move my body movements, and my right arm suddenly began to jerk uncontrollably. I was conscious but all I could hear faintly was my kids screaming and a loud whooshing sound as If a helicopter in my ear and a huge migraine that had gone on for weeks before. Finally, a few seconds later I was able to whisper and grab out to reach my husband for help. I was rushed to the ER once again and they ran all sorts of tests, and nothing showed up. My driving was restricted for months, and I was referred to a neurologist. I questioned God because my independence was being stripped away from me. What lesson was he trying to teach me? I had to have someone drive me to doctor's appointments to take my children to school and I absolutely hated it because when I needed my husband there to do those things I thought that things wouldn't be done right. I was forced to lay down my baggage and not only trust him but trust God. I was in a constant state of negativity, and I told myself that it could have been a stroke, that it was epilepsy, and I'd never get to drive again. What about acting? What about my new job? I've only worked there for a week and I'm already having to take a leave of absence. I had to lean on God and not my own understanding. I had multiple EEG's, an ambulatory EEG, a CT scan, sleep tests and the doctors couldn't find anything. I was extremely stressed, and sleep deprived and that took my anxiety levels to an all-time high. Which led me to having a partial seizure or a stressed induced seizure. My emotions were always going from zero to one hundred, I always felt over stimulated and often depressed. I knew my family history of mental health and I felt like I needed to do more searching within myself. I went and requested to speak with a doctor about testing to see if there were any signs of neurodivergence. You hear people speak all the time about mental health and you think that it's always someone that has special needs or is bipolar but mental health has many layers. I began to look into my symptoms. In my research, things kept coming up about ADHD and autism. I was in complete denial because no one was about to tell me something was wrong with me. I've already had a psychiatrist diagnose me with anxiety and depression. They attempted putting me on medication and I absolutely hated it. So, someone telling me something else was wrong with me was going to send me into another world wind. I didn't want to take any more medication, I just wanted to feel normal but all the things that I have felt internally, and all the impulsive behavior have been there since I was a child. I would get angry and tear things up and throw things at my sister. I would flip out on my children if I got too overstimulated. If there is too much information for me to process at one time I would get frustrated and storm off or even just sit there and break down in tears. To other people on the outside looking in it may look like this girl has some real issues and I truthfully I really did have issues. I was just too afraid and too prideful to admit it. I was always the one complaining that I never got to do anything for myself, and this was the one thing I needed to do for myself...get help. I finally buckled down and went and got tested for ADHD and my numbers were off the charts. I was asked questions about my emotional state and my mental state and my sleep habits. They even asked me about my childhood and my educational background. I was clinically diagnosed with severe ADHD in November of 2023. I thought that this was going to be the worst thing that has happened to me but actually it's probably the best thing that I have ever done for myself. My whole life I had been fighting a condition that I didn't understand what it was. ADHD is not just someone being hyperactive, aloof or forgetful. Those are just smaller symptoms of a larger issue. There's nothing wrong or bad about me and it's not a disability. My brain just functions differently. Statistically, women and girls are more likely to go undiagnosed because the condition shows up differently than in little boys and men. ADHD is a chemical imbalance in the brain stemming from the pituitary gland and hypothalamus. This is the part of the brain that releases endorphins which are hormones that affect psychological functions such as a regulated mood, emotions, decision making and executive functioning. They are supposed to be released in your body when participating in pleasurable activities such as exercise or a hobby or eating foods such as chocolate. The issue is, a person who has ADHD has a deficiency in endorphins being released so this results in impulsive behaviors that triggers the release of those endorphins for instant satisfaction such as impulsive shopping or spending, or even worse uncontrollable eating habits, drugs and alcoholism, reckless sexual behavior or criminal activity. It also affects my mood and the way that I handle my emotions and now looking back the way I've always reacted in situations could have been handled differently if I were aware of my condition. Growing up, I always knew the kids that were in the special needs classes either had a learning disability or were dealing with some type of mental health challenge. Growing up in the nineties and 2000s, if you had ADHD you were put into the special needs classes, and it was always a negative stigma that you were slow or considered "The R word". One thing that I learned was that ADHD is also a genetic condition that can be passed down from generation to generation. Once I started opening up about my condition I felt things were looking up. Of course, there were some who said all kinds of negative things like "Everybody just wants to talk about they have ADHD now!" or "Just get over it, you are stressing too much!" Oh, and let's not forget the religious saying things like We are not going to touch and agree on that! We are going to pray that demon off of you!" Don't get me wrong I'm definitely an advocate for spiritual warfare and I believe prayer and manifestation works but I also understand science and believe that faith without works is dead. If a doctor tells you that you have a heart condition and you refuse any treatment because you refuse to touch and agree with what the doctor said then that's pointless. You have to pray along with the treatment that the doctor has ordered. I've even had someone say that I was cursed by God because I brought on spirits when I left church. I learned to shut out the misinformed and miseducated and I even had to give up on sharing knowledge with them because people are going to talk about you whether you are doing good or bad. I chose to move differently.

I began to reflect on my life internally and I started to realize that when I was empty, I could no longer expect someone else to fill my cup. I had to learn to love my true authentic self-first before I could love someone else. I grew up and became self-aware so that I don't inflict pain and trauma on other people because of my insecurities. I had to come to terms and forgive myself for the fact that I was bleeding on my children and my husband and everyone else around me. I realized that even though I had mommy issues and daddy issues I couldn't even blame them. I went through a season of isolation during that time where I couldn't drive or go to work. Also, during that time, my grandmother passed, and I was heartbroken, but I knew that she had struggled a long hard life, and she was finally at peace within herself. Her last days she was angry at the world because of why her life ended the way it did. I accepted the fact that once she was gone she didn't live her life in vain. A few weeks after she passed I was asleep, and I heard her voice in my sleep saying "Ciera don't act like that now! Ciera don't do that!" I couldn't see her face. It was almost like she didn't want me to see her. I woke up out of my sleep, but I wasn't afraid. I knew it was her trying to speak to me. I didn't know exactly what it meant but I took it as her way of saying get back up and get it together. Even though she was not what some may consider a traditional grandmother she still taught me things about life. Like, Don't take things in life for granted. Love yourself and learn how to say no. Self-love is the best love and If I don't take care of myself then I'm no good to anyone else around me. One thing I admired about her was that there was no shame in her game. She could care less about what others thought about her. Drug addiction and all she was not afraid to tell the truth. Whatever decisions she made for her life, good or bad she owned it. For the first time in my life, I'm unmasking it all. Not in any malice or means to expose someone else's life but to be real with myself and those around me. I want my story to help someone else in some way because we all have flaws, and we have to learn to embrace those flaws and take life by the horns and ride. Of course, my ride was even a wild ride but every time I got knocked off the bull I got back up and kept pushing. Only this time, I'm taking my life back unapologetically and living it for me.

Chapter 10

Hard Lessons Learned

Every day we wake up and live our lives and subconsciously we have been shaped and molded to become who we are. However, no matter how many masks and costumes we wear and how many roles we portray some of us still wonder who we are at the surface. Somewhere along the way we lost our true identities. We spend our whole lives trying to be people pleasers and putting on these personas that we become characters in a fantasy of our own delusions, while living in a world of reality where everyone is claiming to be real. So, I want to rip the mask off and unveil my truth, my identity and the journey of my own healing.

I've heard many times that accountability is not an attack on one's character and I wholeheartedly agree. However, some of us struggle with the difference between true accountability and their own selfish expectations of how they believe others should live their lives. So, I must question, what are you holding others accountable to? Could it be family traditions, and beliefs? Or could it be the family's status and reputation that you are trying to uphold? Could it be religious beliefs, practices, rituals and traditions? Maybe it's imposing personal beliefs about yourself or personal beliefs about the other person. Often we hold people accountable to things out of good intent. Most of us naturally want the best for those that we love and care for however, we fail to realize that we underestimate others and tend to forget that we have to allow space for people to live their lives on their own terms and make decisions that are best for them. On the other hand, if you are the one that is being held accountable, remember that even though our lives are our own, our lives are really not our own. Every decision that we make affects everyone in our lives whether it be children, or parents or people that we may not even know. So, it's okay to take heed to the advice that our loved ones give us. Just don't let it be the end all be all. We have to find a balance between knowing what advice is best for our lives and personal circumstances. First, seek God and trust his guidance. Secondly, gain an unbiased opinion from someone you trust, maybe a therapist or life coach. Third, weigh out pros and cons to decide what makes sense logically and not based on emotion and remember to weigh the outcomes. Question, who will be affected and how will they be affected? Lastly, make the decisions for you and not anyone else's opinion. At the end of the day, you only have to answer to God and remember whatever you choose there always will be positive or negative consequences and outcomes. We just have to take our losses as hard lessons learned. However, we get so caught up in what others may say, think or feel that we forget what's really best for us because we don't know how to make logical decisions for ourselves. We allow others to make us think that we are a failure without that job or man or whatever you are holding on to. Most of the time, it's because we are trying to put on an image that we have it all together and in reality we are hanging on by a thread. We have to remember that our lives were already destined before we were even born so why do we allow others and naysayers divert us from the path and purpose that we are already supposed to be walking in? We often see this with our parents, family members, church members or anyone who is close to us. Particularly ones who are in some form of authority over us. We know that most times they have had more experiences in life, and they were the ones that raised us. Sometimes they know us more than we know ourselves but as you grow and learn and get to certain stages in life, you evolve, and you are more than likely not the same person you were in your youth. You begin to have your own life experiences, your mindset and understandings begin to change and always remember no one really knows the whole you except the one who created you.

My whole life I was buried under the weight of others' opinions of me. I was suffocating myself in silence and putting pressure on myself to meet society's and my family's expectations. A lot of those expectations were unrealistic and irrational. I've had to grow and heal from the guilt of not living my life according to others' standards. I recently saw a post on social media, it was a meme of a man standing in a prison cell and he was locking himself in this cage bar by bar and brick by brick. Each bar and brick represented someone else's expectation or someone else's opinion. The caption stated, " I feel like I'm in a prison only other people's opinions are the bars" On the outside looking in, it looks as if I have an " I don't care" attitude or it may even seem selfish to some but take a look within yourself and ask, what is it within me that bothers me about the decision that someone makes? Do I doubt that they will be successful? Am I fearful that they will hurt themselves or someone else? Out of good intentions we want what's best for those that we love and care for yet, in life we have to learn to set boundaries for ourselves not only to protect our peace but also for ourselves to understand that we are valuable no matter which path we take in life. Our brokenness and mistakes we make don't define us. It's just hard lessons learned in life. If we allow others to choose our path for us then we will have no room to learn or grow. I remember when my daughters were babies, I was teaching them to walk. It would hurt me so much to see them fall and cry especially if they got hurt. I wanted to run to pick them up and sometimes catch them before they would fall. Pretty soon, they would cry when they fell and sat there until I came to pick them up from their fall. That showed me that If I kept picking them up they would never learn to pick themselves up. The same thing applies in life with the ones we love. We have to allow room and grace for our loved ones to grow. However, if you see someone heading towards a path of destruction, you have every right to guide them to what is right but just like the old saying goes. "You can bring a horse to the water, but you can't make them drink." I know it's hard to watch someone make a decision that could potentially cause them hurt or danger and every decision we make in life affects everyone around us in some way, but it is still the choice that we have to accept. In a world where everyone is inauthentic, living life day to day in a facade. We have to find the courage to be our true selves flaws and all unapologetically. I was driving down a long back road one night and as I was in deep thought, I challenged myself with the question, morally and in the eyes of God and the universe, what is frowned upon more? How we treat ourselves, or how we allow others to treat us? I began to realize that what makes God and the universe more angry is when we lower our values and standards to appease others and even more when we throw away our moral and spiritual compass out of anger to intentionally inflict pain on others. I learned that impulsive decisions out of emotion are dangerous. It is vital to think through and process our emotions not only for the safety and wellbeing of others but also our safety, mental and physical well-being and those closest to us. I truly believe that we walk out of the path that we are designated in life because we simply cannot find gratitude in the life that we are given. We don't see our worth and we second guess the gifts, the capabilities and intellectual abilities that God gave us. It is a disgrace to our creator and our own existence when we second guess our purpose. I truly believe we are brought into life for different reasons. To learn spiritual lessons for this life, to help others and be a testament to someone else's struggle then, to teach and bring healing to help others out of a place of darkness and enlighten them with love and grace. My story is not a story to expose or point fingers at those who may have hurt me but to bring light to the fact that I was brought here to learn lessons and bring light to the truths I had hidden. The way that darkness keeps you entangled is through isolation and silence. They say what's done in the dark eventually comes to the light. So, in order for me to really live life on my own terms is to turn the lights on.

Special Thanks and Credits

Tay Neely Photography, Octavious Neely

Sight 4Ever Photography Troy Williams

Tiffany Williams Greene, Editor

Rona Neely, Editor

Kiyania Brown, Clinical and mental health resources.

https://lp.recoverycentersofamerica.com
(Substance abuse resources)

https://www.thehotline.org
(Domestic Violence Hotline)

https://www.rainn.org/resources
(Sexual abuse and assault resources)

https://ADDitudemag.org

(ADHD/ADD resources)

https://988lifeline.org

(Suicide and Crisis resources)

https://samhsa.gov

(Substance abuse and mental health crisis resources)

About the author

Born in small town Laurens, South Carolina, author and actress Ciera Sharde' Cohen is a wife and mother of two daughters. With her personal experiences she brings a real-world perspective to understanding the truth about trauma and healing. Using her background in creative writing and acting she sheds light on her insight about life, self-love and mental health. She wants to bring the real and raw, to encourage others to be authentic with who they are, unapologetically.

Made in the USA
Columbia, SC
16 February 2025